Love + Green Building

YOU AND ME AND THE BEAUTIFUL PLANET

written by Jason F. McLennan
illustrated by José Luis Gutiérrez Brezmes

Love + Green Building

An Ecotone Publishing Book 2020
Copyright ©2020 Jason F. McLennan

Ecotone Publishing is an Imprint of the International Living Future Institute

All rights reserved. No part of this publication may be reproduced, distributed or transmitted in any form or by any means, including photocopying, recording, or other electronic or mechanical methods, without the prior written permission of the publisher, except in the case of brief quotations embodied in critical reviews and certain other noncommercial uses permitted by copyright law. For permission requests, write to the publisher, addressed "Attention Permissions Coordinator," at the address below.

Ecotone Publishing
1501 East Madison Street, Suite 150,
Seattle 98122

Author: Jason F. McLennan
Illustrator: José Luis Gutiérrez Brezmes
Book Design: Kristina Avramovic Oldani
Edited by: Fred McLennan

Library of Congress Control Number: 2020934490
Library of Congress Cataloging-in Publication Data
ISBN: 978-0-9972368-8-0

A slightly different version of this text originally appeared in Transformational Thought II, ©2016 by Jason F. McLennan under the title A Sustained Awakening of the Human Heart: Love and Green Building.

A related version was reprinted in Arcade Magazine, Issue 35.1 under the title
A Sustained Awakening of the Human Heart: Love and Green Building.

1. Architecture   2. Environment   3. Family

Printed in Canada, processed chlorine-free, using vegetable-based ink.

"To my children, Rowan, Aidan, Declan, and Julian in the hopes that they grow up to love the natural world as much as I do."

JASON F. MCLENNAN

"To my children, Mariana and Pablo, reminding them they should strive to become better than me."

JOSÉ LUIS GUTIÉRREZ BREZMES

I practice green building for a simple reason.

Love.

It sounds corny, but it's the truth—and I think it's the truth for many of us in the green building movement.

Why else would we do it when it can sometimes be so difficult?

Typically, we meet considerable resistance—we have to confront people who do not want to do things differently, and we have to fight to make change, which sometimes feels like the opposite of love.

Often, we lose and
we have to compromise.

We take risks—personal and professional—and we have to unlearn and relearn things when it would be so much easier to just do things "the normal way."

I know that some people practice green building for different reasons—for money, for market position, or because others are doing it—and these are okay places to start.

But I think most people are in it for a much more fundamental reason.

We know that the built environment is humanity's largest manifestation. Our biggest impacts on climate and the health of the planet come from our cities and towns and the buildings and homes within them.

We understand that as the planet's population is growing, these negative impacts are expanding.

With a heavy heart we understand that all life support systems around the globe are in decline and that the rate of that decline is increasing.

We see the diminishment of so many places that we love and fear for the places that are next to weaken or disappear altogether.

It is our love that pushes us to sit with the pain of this reality and then act in the ways we have at our disposal.

I do not believe
that some magical
technology or savior
politician will rescue us.

The only thing that can save us is a sustained awakening of the human heart.

This awakening is required to return our species to where we belong as an essential, integral part of our beautiful, wonderful, amazing planet—
not separate from the natural world, and certainly not "above it" as the dominating entity. That's not love—it's ego.

When you love something, you want to take care of it—
to preserve it and ensure its well-being through time.

I love my children like this, but love can extend outward in powerful ways beyond our families to other things.

And when you love a place, you want to take care of it too.

Some people pursue green building for very personal reasons. They love their children and grandchildren and understand that leaving them a healthy future is essential.

They understand that environmental impacts, including the devastating effects of climate change, are already upon us.

Some people get into green building because they love their communities and the wider networks of people who surround them.

Like many of us, I have seen development destroy the places of my childhood—both natural and man-made.

Like many of us, I am motivated to turn back the tide and take part in regenerating the land, blurring the distinction between the built and natural environments.

Others embrace green building because they see people's health suffering from poor indoor air quality and exposure to toxins. They see loved ones with cancers that are clearly environmentally related and watch as people they care about struggle with allergies and asthma.

I have lost too many people I love to cancer and struggled my entire life with allergies that were likely caused by pollution in my hometown.

People realize that we are surrounded by a spew of toxic chemicals, and without product transparency we cannot even know how to begin eradicating them. If we don't know what's in the things we buy, how can we tell the good from the bad?

Some people get pulled into green building because they also begin to understand that the way we design, build, and operate our buildings often has hidden consequences that hurt the most economically disadvantaged among us.

They begin to connect the dots between the things we use and where they are made. They understand that the majority of the pollution caused by manufacturing ends up affecting people who will never enjoy the fruits of their own labor.

When you dig into it, you realize that you can't have two worlds—the haves and have-nots—and expect to have a healthy future for all.

Economic resilience, ecological resilience, and local self-reliance are all inextricably linked.

It is possible to love people you'll never have the chance to meet. A love for all of humanity drives members of this movement to make change.

Of course there are other people who do this because of a pure love of the wild.

Yes, they love trees and might be inclined to hug them.

Some like to hunt and fish, getting sustenance directly from the natural world.

Others hunt only
with cameras, chasing
rainbows and vistas
of light and dark.

Some spend time in wild places whenever they can while others simply take comfort knowing that wildness is there, protected while they sit safely inside a responsibly made building.

They love other species big and small and see the impacts we are making on habitats the world over—in our forests and swamplands, our oceans and streams. They understand that materials come from somewhere, and toxic releases end up in unintended places.

The rich biological heritage of the planet is under direct and sustained assault, as we mine, clear-cut, and pollute.

If you are like me, you are deeply and profoundly saddened by the world's loss of an incredible heritage of animals and plants and other creatures too small to notice.
It is sad to think that my grandchildren will likely never see a polar bear or a rhino or a tiger.

We who practice green building know in our guts that paving over wetlands and forests—even farmland and pasture—is moving us deeply into dangerous ground and diminishing who we are as a people. We feel the dull pain of suburbia eating the country and the endless, insatiable demand for cheap goods and cheap thrills.

Some people express their love of the Earth and all that inhabit it through their faith, and they know that how we are currently living goes against the grain of their beliefs.

Can you believe in something greater than what we understand without acknowledging the interconnectedness of everything?

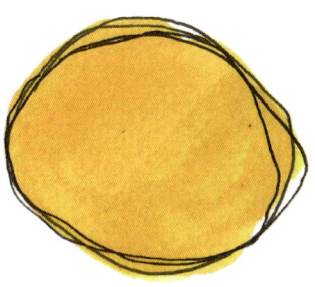

Oh yes, it will take a sustained awakening of the human heart to recognize kinship with all species—to realize that what we do to them we do to ourselves. We need a heartfelt understanding that to do otherwise is morally wrong.

The good news is that more of us awaken each year.

We accept that there are things, people, places, and creatures big and small that we care for passionately and that are worth fighting for.

We join similar movements that have yet to be united, but whose roots are dug equally deep into the soil of caring.

Much of what I'm talking about here could apply to sustainable agriculture and organic farming, to social justice movements or environmentalism generally. We have different areas of focus, but we are all acting from a place of love.

It is time we collaborate and come together. We need new tools, new systems, and, most of all, new stories that properly frame our humanity and our civilization within a truly sustainable, regenerative future.

So we practice green building because it's an actionable way to express our love where the impacts are largest and the effects most evident—in the very places where we live and work. We work on green buildings because it's the only responsible thing to do.

I take heart that beautiful people like you care deeply and are trying to make change regardless of how hard it may seem to be.

I appreciate it
and I love you for it.

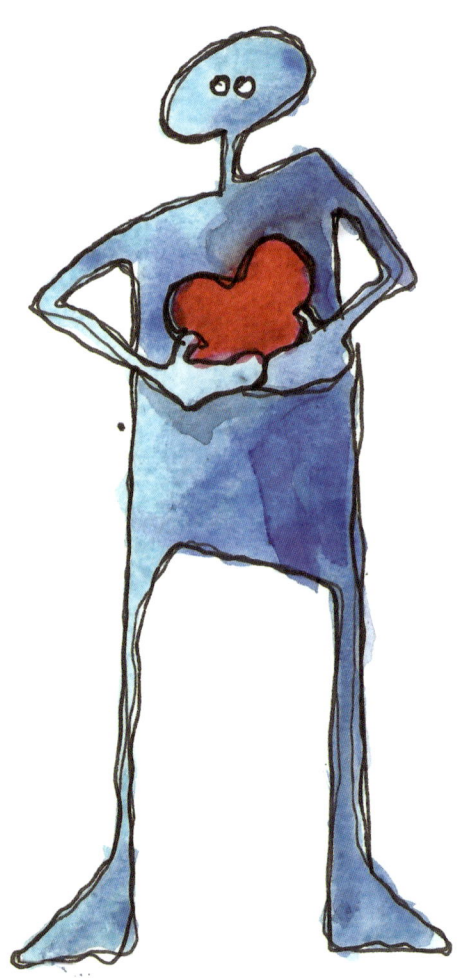

about the author

Considered one of the world's most influential individuals in the field of architecture and the green building movement today, Jason McLennan is a highly sought out designer, consultant, and thought leader around the planet. He is the recipient of the prestigious Buckminster Fuller Prize (the planet's top prize for socially responsible design). He has been called the "Steve Jobs" of the green building industry, a "World Changer" by GreenBiz magazine and has been selected as the Award of Excellence winner for Engineering News Record—one of the only individuals in the architecture profession to have won the award in its 55-year history.

McLennan is the creator of the Living Building Challenge—the most stringent and progressive green building program in existence, as well as a primary author of the WELL Building Standard, which is sweeping the globe. He is the author of six books on Sustainability and Design—used by thousands of practitioners each year, including the Philosophy of Sustainable Design, which is considered the "bible" for green building—and he is both an Ashoka Fellow and Senior Fellow of the Design Future's Council. He has been selected by Yes! Magazine as one of 15 people shaping the world and works closely with world leaders, Fortune 500 companies, leading NGO's, major universities, celebrities and influential development companies—all in the pursuit of a world that is socially just, culturally rich and ecologically restorative. He is the founder of the International Living Future Institute and he is the CEO of McLennan Design—his own architectural and planning practice, designing some of the world's most advanced green buildings. McLennan's work has been published in dozens of journals, magazines and newspapers around the world.

about the illustrator

José Luis Gutiérrez Brezmes is the former president and founding partner of Sustainability for Mexico A.C. SUME, Established Council for Mexico of the World Green Building Council. He is Director of the Department of Architecture, Urbanism and Civil Engineering of the Universidad Iberoamericana in Mexico City.

With more than twenty-five years of professional experience in the areas of design and construction, he has specialized in the issues of sustainable building and accessibility for people with disabilities.

international living future institute

The International Living Future Institute (ILFI) is a hub for visionary programs. ILFI offers global strategies for lasting sustainability, partnering with local communities to create grounded and relevant solutions, including green building and infrastructure solutions on scales ranging from single room renovations to neighborhoods or whole cities. ILFI administers the Living Building Challenge, the world's most rigorous and ambitious performance standard, as well as the Living Product Challenge and Living Community Challenge. In addition, ILFI offers transparency labels through JUST, Declare, and Reveal. Zero Energy and Zero Carbon certification, and Living Future Accreditation are also available. Additionally, ILFI is home to Ecotone Publishing, a unique publishing house dedicated to telling the story of the green building movement's most innovative buildings, thinkers and practitioners.

ecotone publishing

Founded by green building experts in 2004, Ecotone Publishing is dedicated to meeting the growing demand for authoritative and accessible books on sustainable design, materials selection and building techniques in North America and around the world. Ecotone searches out and documents inspiring projects, visionary people, and innovative trends that are leading the design industry to transformational change toward a healthier planet.

mclennan design

McLennan Design is one of the world's leading regenerative design firms and focuses on deep green outcomes in the fields of architecture, planning, consulting and product design. The firm uses an ecological perspective to drive design creativity and innovation—reimagining and redesigning for positive environmental and social impact.

Founded by global sustainability leader and green design pioneer Jason F. McLennan and joined by partner Dale Duncan, the firm was formed with a clear overarching purpose—to make a significant positive change in the world, with a particular focus on deep green, regenerative design solutions as their means. The firm exists to be a change agent, using design and consulting as a powerful tool for transformation. As the founder and creator of many of the building industry's leading programs including the Living Building Challenge and its related programs, McLennan and his design team bring substantial knowledge and unmatched expertise to the A/E industry. The firm's diverse and interdisciplinary set of services makes for a culture of holistic solutions and big picture thinking.

other books by jason f. mclennan

ZUGUNRUHE: THE INNER MIGRATION TO PROFOUND ENVIRONMENTAL CHANGE
by Jason F. McLennan

THE PHILOSOPHY OF SUSTAINABLE DESIGN
by Jason F. McLennan

TRANSFORMATIONAL THOUGHT: RADICAL IDEAS TO REMAKE THE BUILT ENVIRONMENT
by Jason F. McLennan

TRANSFORMATIONAL THOUGHT II: MORE RADICAL IDEAS TO REMAKE THE BUILT ENVIRONMENT
by Jason F. McLennan

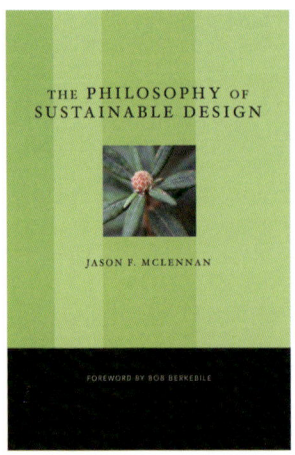